Step into a sacred space where poems become prayers and whispers become revelations.

Whispers of His Word is a tender and powerful collection of spiritually inspired poetry that journeys through brokenness into healing.

Restored and radiant, each poem invites readers to sit quietly with the Lord, hear His voice, and walk deeper into the light of His Truth.

Whether read in stillness or aloud in fellowship, *Whispers of His Word* is an invitation and spark for rekindled faith.

Author's Message

I didn't set out to write a book. I was simply sitting with the Lord during a particularly difficult season, opening my heart in quiet moments. As I reflected on Scripture and allowed His presence to meet me there, words began to pour out—honest, unpolished, and deeply personal. What followed was a collection born not of planning but of prayer.

These pages carry the weight of whispered revelations, tearful prayers, and commitments made in the stillness. Many poems emerged from sacred encounters, when I felt God spoke directly to the deepest part of me. They are not just writings; they are testimonies.

My faith is the cornerstone of who I am. It teaches me to be kind, listen, and notice others. My love for children and my desire to write for them directly result from my relationship with the Lord. But *Whispers of His Word* is for anyone seeking to be reminded that we are not alone.

This book is a story of being seen, known, and unconditionally loved by a God who knows every part of us, yet still calls us His child.

Blessings,
Bette Saffran

In quiet moments, His voice can be heard

These are the whispers that carry us—gentle truths, sacred nudges, a Savior's love made known in stillness.

Whispers of His Word

BETTE SAFFRAN

Whispers of His Word

ISBN: 978-1-965142-42-4 (Paperback)
ISBN: 978-1-965142-43-1 (Hardback)

Library of Congress LCCN: 2025909510

When Did I Meet Jesus

When Did I Meet Jesus?

I was exposed to church as a young child. All four of us were seated on the front pew, flanked on either side by Mom and Dad. Did I meet Jesus then? Only as a child, I may have learned of Him in Sunday school. I knew at Christmas we were celebrating the birth of Jesus. But what did that mean? Rebirth and renewal meant nothing to me as a young child. Christmas was presents, and that's how we celebrated Jesus's birth... so yay for Jesus. But once Christmas was done and all the presents were no longer new, then what did Jesus mean? Then came Easter, and Jesus was once again being celebrated. I had a new Easter dress and white socks and was wearing my sister's patent leather shoes that she had outgrown. But they had a bit of a heel, and that, along with Easter candy and bunnies, made that holiday memorable. Did I meet Jesus then? As life in my home became increasingly difficult, the noise of Jesus was drowned out. I looked at my mother's relationship with Jesus as a shelter for all her troubles and woes. I certainly did not meet Jesus at that time. I was way too cool for all of that.

It wasn't until I remarried that I started attending church again. Tom's dad was a priest, and I loved him a lot, so maybe my heart started to long. I'm still not sure what happened. I went to church with my parents, and my daddy showed me a message in the church bulletin that struck me hard. It said the choir was starting their Broadway Show dinner theater again for the next year. I know now that I met Jesus because he spoke straight to me that day.

I set my calendar to show up for choir and never looked back again. Did I meet Jesus for the right reason, or was he filling a void in my life?

He has his ways of doing both, and that's what he did that year. I sang with the choir and started writing, directing, and producing the show. We did a show each year I was there, and funny, when I left, they stopped. I realize now, with what I know about Him, there must not have been one left with that void. I met Jesus and took him with me from that point on, wherever I went.

Jesus saw to my needs and never asking much of me. He's selfless and continues to give. Who would have thought I'd do Broadway in church, but He never stopped there. Now that I'm older, I know I've met Jesus in all my life situations. I'm unsure my testimony is much of a draw, as most won't relate to my story.

He's shown up in so many places since then. He was there when my granddaughter was born and when my daughter had an illness. He was still there as life turned inside out when my granddaughter had her trials.

But none so bold and intense as right now. I'm sure his intensity has always been with me; I never felt it so strongly. He's teaching me, as the Messiah, something new each passing day. I'm listening and writing as I know to do, just trying to keep up. I know he has a purpose I'm not ready to find out what it is. But I know I meet Jesus every night right here and he teaches me once again.

High Expectations

High Expectations

Expectation of life's elations crashing to the ground...
It whirls around us as anticipation surrounds us, no satisfaction found.
Where's that happy ending? The light and tunnel at very least to pretend...
How can something so amazing leave emptiness of heart, unfathomed...
Excitement builds as though nothing more can be seen apart from this dream in motion.
To end this dream in motion
Is this how it's written this story and journey
Heart beating with expectation for release
Those close unable to see or possibly believe
this feeling so empty and desperate void of dream
close, even closer, not able to relieve the feeling of ending, having no good
a time to be amazed and floating, if even for a time
lack of understanding, this incomprehensible measurement in space.
Spinning out of control, sinking down deeper away for the joy and attention expected
The darkness envelopes the light, fading further
Unseeing, unsettling blindness ensuing darkness accepted.

Fishers of Men

The needy are not inside; are we preaching to the choir
Jesus made us fishers of men that won't be found within
Within hallowed halls of rusty doors where hinges need be
removed

Within safely close-knit friends of faith that already know the
truth
Fishers of men from outside our walls that Jesus died to save
A drop of His blood shed for all regardless not withstanding
creed or ethinicity.
Why do we insist we still don't know what God is calling us to
task
Are we convinced that there's a higher calling and we must wait
to precieve

Our sedentary determination to wait for a miracle to appear
What do we expect that God has planned more loftier to
appease?
Our skewed confusion of why we're here, in community, faithful
destiny.
God's Kingdom draws near, He appeals to his flock
to serve the least of these

Eyes That See

Eyes That See

All around are hurt and anger,
Pathetic way of peace and love .
Huge hole gaping straight to self
Eyes that never see.

People walking, dirty feet treading,
crusted heart exhausted with every mile.
expectations with little answers from hope,
no knowledge of how or why,
looking not seeing, filthy from coming
Mother and her child.

Not to be seen through pitied eyes that see fully missing the
meaning they send.
Joyous needs, triumphant beginning now littered below piles of
trash, void within.
Making excuses or lack of response in answer to the least of
these?
Personal, abandoned so unadorned, the artifacts of long-ago
dreams.

No longer the search for glorious expectations
Brought low with humanity's greed.
Proving now for all time no room for your past,
And only one has eyes that will see.

Unwilling to see through accepting eyes,
Where life exists in full
Searching deep the eyes of those that come the stab of
perceptible pull.

Do we weep for the loss of humanity.
Failing to listen, voice resounding from a breeze
Refusing to listen yet anxious to hear,
From the only eyes willing to see.

Love Letter from Jesus to Me

Love Letter from Jesus to Me

On this rock I will build my church, for the God of your Father Abraham has revealed who I am. On your own, you have no wisdom that I haven't given to you. You are not original, there is nothing new under the sun, nor am I new. I was there when the cornerstone was laid. My Father and I created this world and all that is in it. That includes you, and I have been waiting ever since for this reality to become a part of you.

Your life has been a façade and nothing real has entered it. You must know and trust I who have made you. I created you in your mother's womb and birthed you into existence. You have been with me all along my child, and I'll never let go of you.

I understand how hard your life has seemed. It's okay if you don't remember people from your past; you must remember me only, but you must remember me continually, never forgetting that I was before you, behind you, and to your side at all times.

I sing over you—how else are you able to create? How many times have you asked me to carry you to the mountain to rest in my arms as you sleep? Even when you were sure you were alone, you never were. I will not leave or forsake you no matter what your mind might tell you. Messages like these are never from me. Any message that tells you that you are on your own only comes from the evil that is on this earth, or it may come from your own heart. Why is your heart hardening around those that I love so completely?

As I formed you, I formed them, and they too are my children, and I love them just as I love you. I am their Father. Write loving things about my children and pray that no matter the circumstances, your heart remains with me until the day I come in triumph and bring you back home with me forever—but you will be among the very ones that you are now having so much trouble loving. My child, you cannot allow this world and your life to turn your heart from me.

What would it be like if Jesus spoke a word to you, if you were the one who answered His question: "Who do you say I am?" asked the teacher far-reaching. Simon Peter said, "The Holy Son Of God, The Great I Am."

Well done, Peter, a miracle—you've been given eyes that see. For only God in Heaven could reveal what you just said about me.

Are You There... See Me Now

Are You There... See Me Now

Today is not as it should be... from behind, it follows me
This life I thought was safe... no longer safe for me
You know all my thoughts
You know my broken heart
When my heart breaks, is your heart broken too?
I have to know, so I ask now: Am I safe with you
Should I trust you with this fragile life
Are you there just watching
No more tears, they're all cried out, why do they keep on falling
I need your strength; I need your peace
I know you see, but do you hear me calling
Can you see me now
through the cracks of life somehow
Am I the one you thought that I would be
Through my hurt and tears, anger and fears
If I step too far, I might fall away
Is this the way you planned my day today

Repentence

Repentance

As though I'm walking with each step
Mud climbs higher up my leg
Until no longer able to move
My words no longer with power
The only way to change must come from outside my own
As I'm broken down and with each break
wounds of sin flow fourth
Replaced by lightness, freedom to move
That comes with every force
Without your light, I'm frozen in time
As the mud that hardens my heart
I fear moving, not allowing for the healing
Out of desperation, I need
Praise for the brokenness not beautiful
But brutal, ugly hard work
You are faithful to do
With every strike, your crucifixion I join
Able to move once more
last shatter and crack, is heard as my soul freedom speed
escapes
Gone from the cell of worldly affection into your open arms
No longer a prisoner no jail cell awaiting
Haste the day when I'm gone

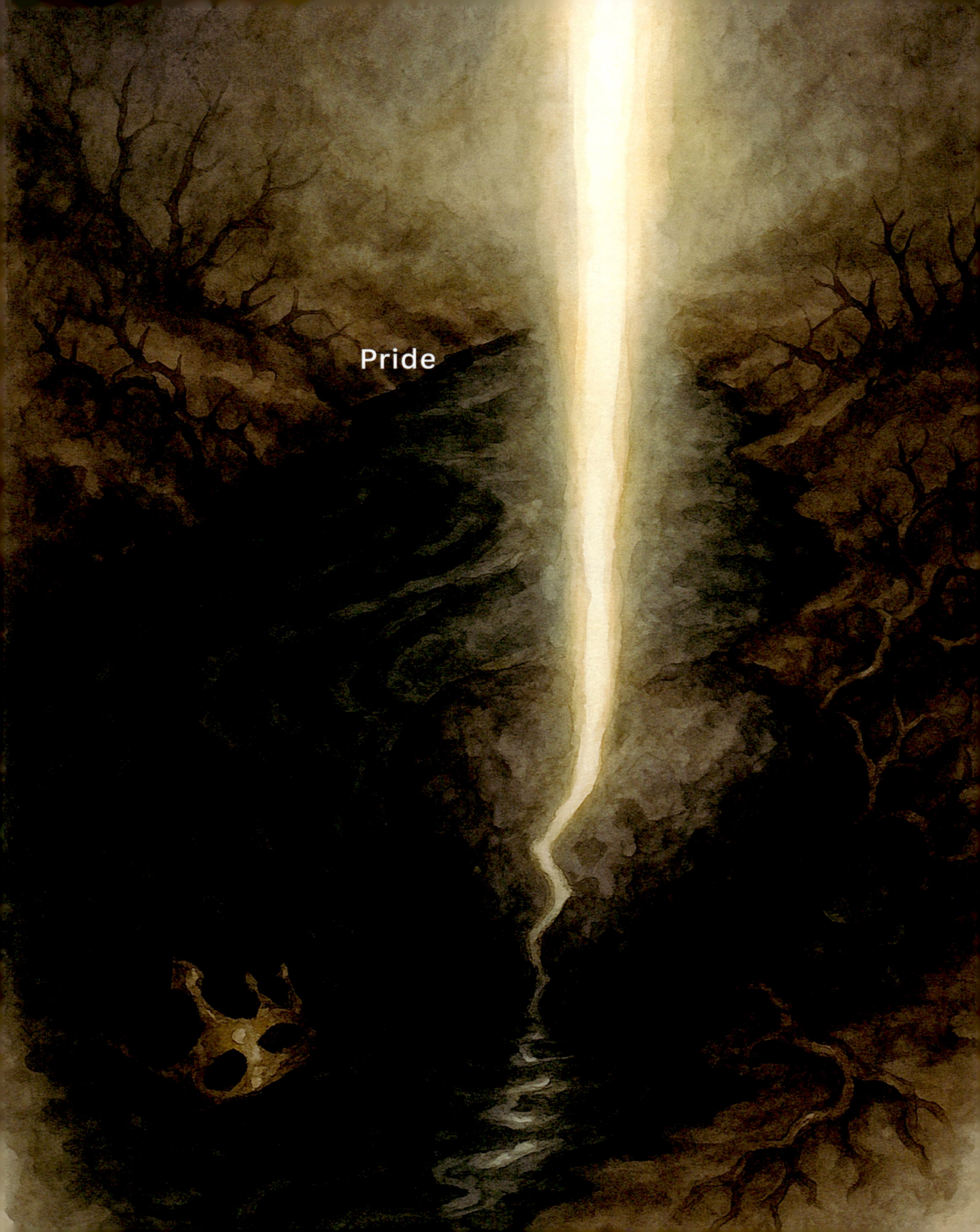

Pride

It's lurking, dark, and ugly
Oozing from beneath its store
Illumined by light, it would bleed and puddle
An odor putrid through life beating its own
Receding for its true reason
A non-repentant world would approve
Jesus, true light, forgive me, rid me from this foul
Your river of living water is dark!
By sin is running dry

Savior part the darkness, empty the abyss to dry
Cleansing as a mighty tide
Darkness to light again.
No other chance to loose it
The weight lying heavy of heart
Odor too acrid alone to stand
Pray ... deliver a top ... your river of life!
And empty me upon your dry land.

Calloused Heart
(producing a crop)

Bette Saffran

Calloused Heart (producing a crop)

Visible, constant reminder, seeing but not to be seen.
Eyes affixed to the next best step, do I have a part...
overlooking, anxious light to green distinguish the chance
that I'd be seen...
With this callous heart.
Inundated through saturation of humanities overexposure.
My heart and soul shut down, unwilling to hear the need
and accept
the still small voice of God.
Staggering urgency with hearts rhythmic beat, palatable,
deafening grows stronger.
Guilt seeps deep, where will he sleep...
Are there children somewhere alone, and scared, waiting
for their father.
Will meager means bring sustenance, enough to build the
body,
Laughter to enrich the soul
How will he know that God adores, with each step he
takes...
Along his broken road.
If not from us profoundly seeing,
still convincing, that we don't.
God will find a way for the least of these,
God will, even when we won't.

Beautifully Broken Ugly and Seeping

Beautifully Broken Ugly and Seeping

My deepest desire is to be broken by God
Cracked as darkness hides
My sin is deep and deeper still
In your faithfulness I hear you cry
Break cut deep and jagged where sin feels safe to
hide
Calloused eliminating light
Where darkness is not shy
Penetrate cracks much deeper
As they draw in themselves to close
Jesus pierce the darkened sin, more filthy in repose
On my own forms hard unyielding
Practiced to run and hide
In pretense the fantasy made real
In deep disturbing pride
Lord break wide for holy light, where darkness can
not hide.
The sin now film once hardened
This heart in you is peeled
Redefined! Holy light of hope!
Once layered, laid bear, revealed

The Ranger's Light

The Rangers Light

Light revealed from darkness, pathways streaming as light
is beaming ahead
Dark surroundings all-encompassing loneliness, eyes that
won't see.
Never dark as light coming, you are my light, my darkness
suppressive

Unnecessary wasteful time and thoughts, as the ranger
ahead shines his flashlight high
Do we still miss the light, finding the dark in the glow that
has come to save

From darkness into light follow the light the darkness
staggering, immobile,
How to see if now through darkened eyes. Steps unmoving,
to loose unyielding
Perception lost in darkness without a sound

Head below the earth to cover, ignore no light can shine
Eyes that are poor unable to see or unwilling to
understand

Shining forever to brighten a path, a path that meets the
light of a stranger
To walk not alone eyes bright from the light, within no
darkness, atoned.
Bearing all accepting all now lovely perception,
enthralling, the light of the ranger.

Belonging

Belonging

Now old, how young a baby an old man and young alike
there belonging and moving forward to feel the warmth
and comfort of the illumined path

Yet what to greet at end a flicker of feeling in a world
become so dark
To pass in and out as boats atop of sea of moving, yet so
immobile
To feel to hear to find to thought, that care is passing by
A light to search to find our journey to guide us back to
shore

Still in and out not sure of belonging Light continues to
shine.
A lighthouse beaming just off shore
Life convincing nothing to see nothing to find
Through darkness so hard , to see knowing and feeling
A light but nothing more.

Why detest and ignore the other, dark eyes not seeing
a light flickering through night
Still speck of light off shore, borne to protect, love and
support,
it beckons , stare hard with open eyes and bursting heart

Join in the light belonging, not just accepted embraced,
Accepting the other's in and outs
light stronger now belonging,
eyes filled with light no apathy nor dark remains.

Called

I've been called and am called
Still of small whisper of breeze
Or the sound of a hurricane bending the trees
Slapping forward to hear to listen and respond
No small sound as a roar was the groan and pleads
The deepest of waves as desires are known
Riding above before a mighty undertow
Calling atop to the valley below
The time has come it's near as close as a message in an
ancient bottle
Crafted from ruins far and between
A reminder of a call from the depth of my being
Say no more simply come be washed and be cleaned

The Bulb

The Bulb

Afresh new life as a bulb raised from beneath, to be robed in
beauty with colored fragrance clothed for release.
Nurtured through rays of sunshine watered to his very core...
Lifting his head, a baby from nest, still safely nestled beneath.
Then A cry cracks through the winter air unattended
No one to see nor hear.

No trace of color nor fragrance his father intended...
The world stale and putrid yet all must be saved...
As the Mighty Nurturer's back was turned
The tender bulb alone bruised and broken ... was cut down and
slain.

Then there within a drift of snow a mighty wind began to blow
It groans as the lost bulb is brought to life with its almighty arms
wrapped round him.

Yet there where he slumps...
beneath the snow slowly yet assuredly...
melting with the bulbs emitting glow...
It rises again scented colors once more...
In the arms of the magnificent nurturer.
The bulb with absolute power dealt the deciding blow to
infinity...
all stale and putrid freely offered ... Magnificent Eternity.

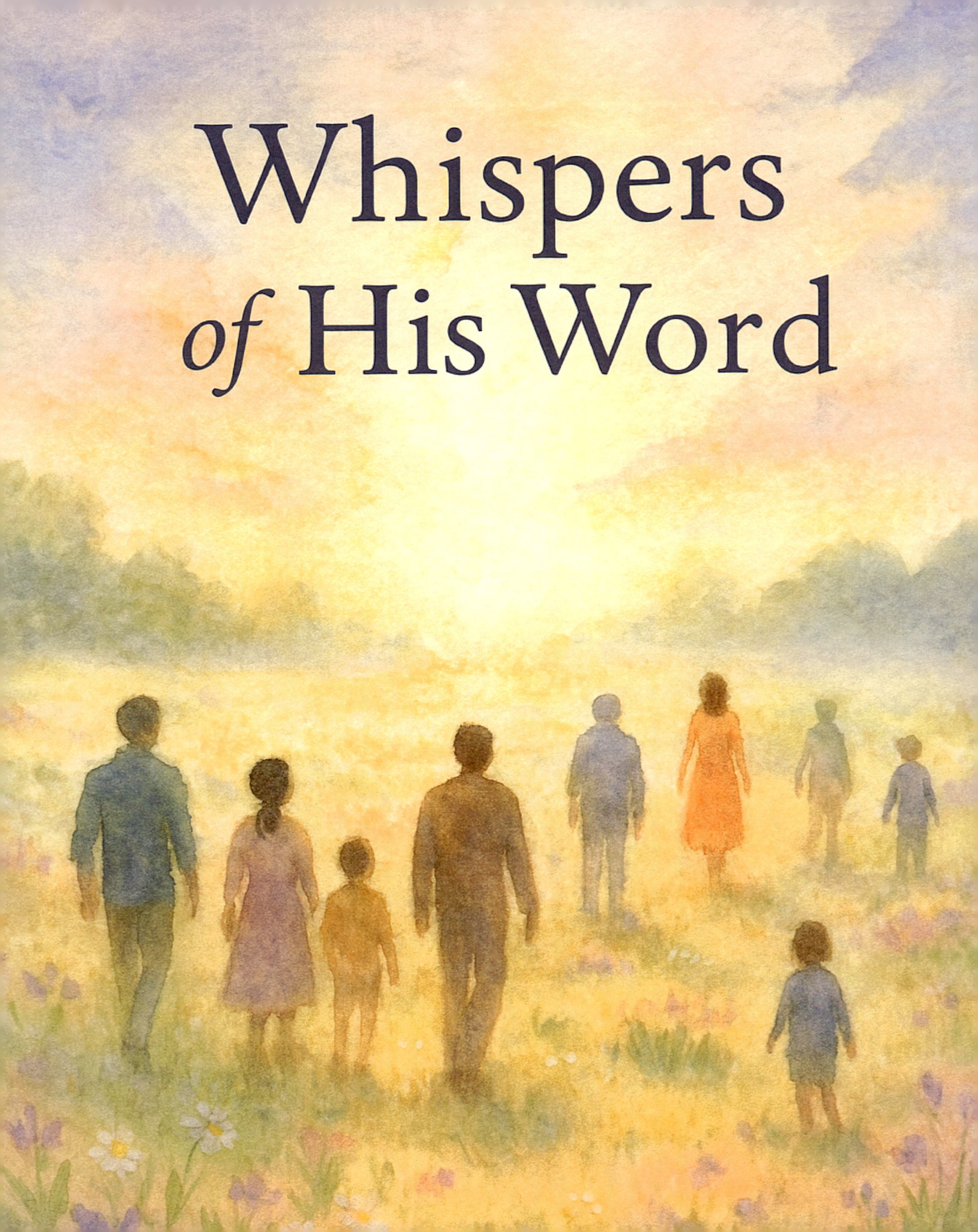

Whispers
of His Word